Original title:
Island Memories

Copyright © 2025 Creative Arts Management OÜ
All rights reserved.

Author: Juliette Kensington
ISBN HARDBACK: 978-1-80581-586-0
ISBN PAPERBACK: 978-1-80581-113-8
ISBN EBOOK: 978-1-80581-586-0

An Ebbing Away

The waves came in with a giggle,
Chasing crabs away with a wiggle.
My hat flew off, oh what a sight,
A seagull dove, it took flight!

I tried to catch it with a dance,
But tripped on sand, no second chance.
Laughter echoed, a silly parade,
As I flopped and flailed in the shade.

The sunburned tourists, oh so bright,
Wore socks with sandals, quite a fright!
They posed for photos with goofy grins,
As the tide rolled in, oh where it's been!

With each retreat, the memories splashed,
Of laughter, mishaps, and ice creams crashed.
A slow dance between sand and sea,
In a world where joy was just to be.

Beneath the Surface

A fish once wore a bright bow tie,
It danced and twirled, oh my, oh my!
A crab with swag joined in the show,
Said, "Watch my moves, I'm quite the pro!"

The octopus poured drinks with flair,
Spilling cocktails everywhere!
The seaweed waved like fans in glee,
As all the critters sang out, "We're free!"

Symphony of the Shore

The seagulls squawked a tune so sweet,
While crabs performed a tap dance feat.
A rogue wave crashed, took out the stage,
But laughter grew, we turned the page!

The sandcastles loomed, a competition,
But left our dreams in a state of demolition.
We built them high, then watched them fall,
And laughed as each one plopped, one and all!

Forgotten Coves

In a cove where the sun forgot,
We found a treasure—an old flip-flop!
It belonged to a pirate, or so we thought,
Now it's a planter, how clever! Not!

The seagulls perched, they seemed to know,
That treasure was just an old work shoe, though.
We shrugged and made a feast by the bay,
With sandwiches that had a tad too much mayo, hooray!

A Hidden Paradise

A turtle wore a pair of shades,
Declaring himself the king of charades.
He challenged us to a race so grand,
But fell asleep, buried in the sand!

A coconu tre fell with a plop,
Francesca dove, yelling, "Stop!"
Yet from the fruit, we brewed a drink,
And laughed till the sun began to sink!

The Call of Distant Horizons

Seagulls squawk, I think they laugh,
My sunscreen's gone – oh what a gaffe!
A crab steals fries right from my plate,
I wave, he scuttles – it's quite the fate.

The waves crash down, they tickle my toes,
But watch out! Here comes a fish that blows!
He splashes me good, I wipe my face,
In this wacky chatter, I find my place.

Patches of Paradise

The hammock swings, a nap is due,
But I'm joined by a parrot too!
He squawks my secrets to the breeze,
And I play it cool like it's a tease.

I grab a snack – a coconut treat,
But a monkey thinks it's quite the feat!
He swings on by, snags my delight,
Now we're both fighting – what a sight!

Secrets of the Lagoon

The water sparkles like my dreams,
I take a dip, hear fishy schemes!
They giggle bubbles, what a joke,
I think I've made aquatic folk!

Splashing around with goofy grace,
A sea turtle joins this funny race,
We swim in circles, what a show,
With laughs that echo, watch us go!

Remnants of a Tropical Dream

I wake up sandy, hair a mess,
My flip-flops gone! Oh, what distress!
A crab's got one, it must be fate,
As I chase him, I can't relate!

A sunset paints the sky so bright,
But my dinner's flying out of sight!
A squirrel dove in, swiped my fries,
In this wild chaos, laughter lies!

Whispers of the Tides

The waves tell secrets with a splash,
As crabs dance by in a hurried dash.
The sun wears sunglasses, oh so bright,
While gulls giggle on their flight.

A sandcastle prince stands tall and proud,
Yet a toddler's foot leaves him cowed.
The tide's got jokes, it pulls and tugs,
That floating flip-flop gives us hugs.

Sunsets in My Soul

Orange and pink paint the evening sky,
While mosquitoes form a social guy.
I sip on lemonade with a twist,
Then I remember that I forgot the list.

My hat flew off and chased a kite,
As sand got in my snack, what a sight!
The sunset grins, it knows my plight,
Even the seagulls can't stop their bite.

Forgotten Shores of Yesteryear

I walked the shore in flip-flop flops,

Gathering shells, but then I lost drops.

A fishy friend leaped high but fell,

In laughter both of us could tell.

My grandma's tales of treasure chests,

Turned to tall tales, no one confessed.

The laughter echoes through the haze,

Of sunburnt noses and sandy days.

Echoes of Seagulls and Sand

Seagulls serenade while I snack and play,

But they're eyeing my fries in a sneaky way.

They cackle and squawk, a feathered band,

As my sandwich slips from my hand.

The sand is warm, it sticks like glue,

It's in my hair and inside my shoe.

Each grain a memory, swirling around,

In a comedy show, on this sandy ground.

Beneath the Coconut Trees

I tried to catch a coconut,
But it fell right on my head.
I laughed and danced like a fool,
Now I need an ice pack instead.

The monkeys threw their peels at me,
I dodged like folks in a game.
They chattered and they giggled,
And I'll never be the same.

A crab approached with swagger,
Pinching my big toe with glee.
I danced away in panic,
Then tripped and fell on three.

Let's gather all our laughter,
And sail it 'round the sea!
For every laugh we capture,
We make our own jubilee.

Lighthouses and Lullabies

A lighthouse winks at midnight,
With a blink that is quite sly.
It sings to all the seagulls,
As they laugh and droop on high.

The waves clap with a playful splash,
While I sip on coconut cream.
A starfish floats by singing,
Turning night into a dream.

I tried to serenade a turtle,
But he just stared in despair.
He muttered something 'bout his sea-mates,
And then vanished in thin air.

The beams of light kept dancing,
While I laughed near the bay.
With every twinkle from above,
I swear, life's a cabaret!

A Driftwood Diary

Found driftwood that seemed to talk,
With tales of beachside fun.
It laughed about the storms it saw,
And how it always won.

I penned my thoughts on sand and shells,
With mama's pen in hand.
A crab read it with a giggle,
Then snapped it up, oh land!

Seagulls tried to steal my book,
Thinking it was just for them.
I chased them off with squeaky shoes,
While they squawked a frantic hymn.

With each wave, my stories twisted,
Like curls in the summer breeze.
A diary full of laughter,
In nature's endless tease.

Memories Written in Salt

I wrote a note upon the shore,
With grains of gleaming white.
But a wave came to claim it,
Sneaky thief in the night.

Gulls laughed at my misfortune,
As I searched for my lost word.
They spun around like dervishes,
And mocked all I had heard.

The salty breeze just danced away,
Taking secrets with the tide.
I shrieked at the horizon,
But the ocean just replied.

So here's to memories unfound,
And laughter shared with all.
For every salty breeze that blows,
We rise, we jump, we fall.

Coral Reef Reverie

Fish with silly grins, they swim about,
Dancing like they have no doubt.
Crabs in tuxedos strut with flair,
Stealing seashells, if you dare!

Gulls caw laughter, swooping low,
Looking for snacks, a quick hello.
The seaweed tickles fishy tails,
As starfish laugh, sharing tales.

A sea cucumber wears a hat,
Wobbles like a drunken cat.
Bubble-blowing dolphins play,
As we splash, hip-hip-hooray!

Underwater parties, oh so bright,
Disco lights in the moonlight.
Jellyfish jive in a wiggly groove,
In this wacky world, we all move!

Dunes of Nostalgia

Footprints lead to nowhere fast,
Memories of moments, forever cast.
Sandcastles crumble, what a sight,
Big waves crash, then take flight.

Seagulls squawk with comic flair,
Stealing fries from our picnic lair.
Sandy toes and sunburnt noses,
Laughing loud as our joy composes.

Kites take off in the gentle breeze,
Tangled in hair, we try to please.
Crabs on parade, marching in line,
Oh, what a world, so silly and fine!

The sun dips low, a golden crown,
As we tumble down to the town.
With jellyfish hats and goofy grins,
These sandy days sure bring wins!

Celestial Skies Over Water

Stars twinkle bright like disco balls,
As we giggle and share our falls.
Moonlight dances on the waves,
Comedic tales of mermaid raves.

Clouds drift lazily, making shapes,
A dragon here? Oh, see those grapes!
The sea whispers jokes from the deep,
We're in stitches, can't help but leap!

Fish throw parties, the ocean's cheer,
Sing songs that only we can hear.
Seashells giggle, rolling their eyes,
In this world, no one ever sighs.

Stars and fish in a cosmic jam,
Expecting us to join—oh, wham!
With every splash, our laughter ignites,
Under celestial skies, what delights!

The Calm After the Storm

Raindrops dance on the sunken sails,
A fishy festival where laughter prevails.
Surfers wipe out, arms flail with glee,
Nature's slip-ups, so wild and free.

Seashells whisper secrets damp,
While sea frogs croak for the damp stamp.
Tides pull back, revealing the fun,
Beachcombers race, let's go for a run!

As puddles form, we leap and splash,
Making waves in a water dash.
And crabs in raincoats join the play,
Dancing by the shore, hip-hip-hooray!

With a rainbow arching high above,
We share some laughs, feel the love.
The calm after chaos, laughter rings,
In this quirky world, joy always clings!

Chasing Shadows on the Beach

Running fast, we slip and slide,
Footprints washed, too quick to hide.
A seagull steals our picnic bait,
We laugh and chase, it's all first-rate.

Laughter echoes, children squeal,
Jumping waves, it's quite the deal.
Sandy hair and sticky toes,
Who knew fun could come from woes?

Dreams Weaved with Sand

Sandcastles built, then washed away,
"Hey, look, mine's taller!" we proudly say.
Towers lean, and walls start to crumble,
We giggle loud, and then we stumble.

Shells in pockets, treasures abound,
In the drift, funny shapes are found.
A crab scuttles, a race begins,
Who knew a pinch could cause such grins?

Stories Told by the Wind

Whispers swirl like cotton candy,
A gust blows, it feels quite dandy.
We claim the tales of salty brine,
Of pirates lost and treasure's shine.

Laughter drifts with a breeze so light,
The sun dips low, it's quite a sight.
Rainbows curl like a dog's long tail,
As we spin yarns, we will not fail.

Where the Ocean Meets the Sky

Waves crash loud, a raucous cheer,
"Surf's up!" we shout, "Come join us here!"
Seagulls swoop with a feathery grace,
While we attempt a graceful embrace.

The horizon blushes with a wink,
We toast to dreams with a salty drink.
With splashes and giggles, we let time slide,
In the sea's embrace, we find our pride.

Castaway Dreams

I built a sandcastle grand,
With a moat and a seashell band.
But the tide came in with a grin,
Now it's just a beachy land.

I found a coconut hat,
To protect me from sun and spat.
Now seagulls all laugh,
As I strut like a cat.

My trusty flip-flops squeak,
They're my unique fashion peak.
But left one on the shore,
The other's on a cheek.

With a fish for my friend,
We swim and giggle, no end.
He tells the funniest tales,
Of bubbles that send.

Between the Waves

Oh, the sun tickles my toes,
As I chase after a hose.
It's just my imagination,
Or are the waves wearing clothes?

Crabs dance with fancy steps,
While I collect seaweed reps.
They pinch me for some fun,
Do they think I'm the chef?

Frogs having a breakdance show,
As I trip on sand and go.
They croak with laughter loud,
And I laugh back, 'Oh no!'

Hula hoops made of sea grass,
I spin them while the time flies past.
But they tangled in my hair,
Now I'm a mermaid, alas!

A Memory in Every Shell

A shell speaks tales so bright,
As I hold it up to the light.
It whispered, 'Don't forget me!'
I said, 'You're quite the sight!'

Found a starfish with a grin,
He said, 'Let the fun begin!'
We starred in a beach movie,
With waves as our twin.

Sand dunes are for rolling fun,
But I tripped under the sun.
I'm now a turtle's pet,
Oh the games that we run!

Seagulls call my name each day,
As I pass them on my way.
They sing with salty cheer,
Just a touch of their play.

The Dawn of a New Journey

The sun woke up with a splash,
Making colors bright and brash.
I waved to the porpoise crew,
They winked with a smile, dashing flash.

With my towel wrapped like a cape,
I'm the hero of my escape.
Fighting off waves with laughter,
In this sandy landscape.

I packed sandwiches with flair,
But a seagull stole my share.
Now I chase him down the beach,
While shouting, 'Hey, that's unfair!'

The tide's a trusty guide,
As I dance along the ride.
Each wave a joke, a nibble,
And I'll surf with pride.

Stargazing Over Waves

The stars above are bright as cheese,
A floating feast, if you please.
We argue if it's dip or spread,
While waves crash softly, dreams in our head.

The moon joins in the silly brawl,
With its glimmering face, it has it all.
We giggle as the tides pull on toes,
Our secret dance, no one else knows.

A lobster sings a silly tune,
While crabs all clap beneath the moon.
The night is young, the laughter loud,
As we stargaze, a silly crowd.

So if you seek a laugh on the shore,
Join us, we've got fun galore.
With friends and waves, all's just right,
As stars and laughter fill the night.

A Poem Written in Sand

With a stick, I scribble my name,
The ocean chuckles, it's quite the game.
Waves wash in like they own the place,
'Bye-bye!' they sing with frothy grace.

Seagulls drop what looks like a treat,
With a caw and a flap, they retreat.
I draw a mermaid who winks and sways,
She gives me a smile, it brightens my days.

A crab sidles up, wearing my shoe,
He laughs at the view, it's odd, but true.
I chase him around, we dance on the line,
A battle of wits, oh, isn't it fine?

The tide comes in, my words disappear,
The ocean giggles, my canvas clear.
But I'll be back with a stick in hand,
More poems to write in the soft, cool sand.

Embraces of the Sea

The sea hugs my toes with a slippery grip,
I stumble and laugh, oh what a trip!
A fish gives me a wink as it swims,
I salute, but my dignity dims.

Driftwood and seaweed, a crown for my head,
I'm a sea king now, just like I said.
But a wave crashes in, my crown floats away,
The fish and I giggle, what a comical display!

Seagulls squawk jokes from their lofty perch,
I roll with laughter, oh what a search.
For treasures hidden in the fine, soft sand,
A rusty old bottle? Why, isn't it grand?

So come to the shore where we laugh and play,
The sea's warm embrace brightens the day.
With waves as our audience, we dance and cheer,
In the silly old world of the salty frontier.

The Melody of Gentle Currents

The waves play a song on the shimmering seas,
A melody sweet carried by the breeze.
I join in tune with a seashell horn,
Making music until the dawn's reborn.

The fish swim by, they're a jolly choir,
Their bubbles pop out, the rhythm goes higher.
I clap my hands, oh, what a show!
The ocean's alive with a splash and a flow.

"Do the crab shuffle!" I shout with delight,
They hop and they scuttle, oh what a sight!
The sand's my stage, the sun starts to rise,
As laughter and joy fill the morning skies.

So if you hear music on a bright sunny day,
Join in the fun, come out to play.
With currents that dance and laughter that bends,
It's a beachside concert that never ends!

Sunsets in a Coconut Shell

A coconut smiled at the sun,
As the day wrapped up its fun.
I tried to take a sip, you see,
But it was just a joke on me.

Splashing waves looked like they danced,
While my flip-flops lost their chance.
Tried to catch a crab with flair,
He pinched my toe, then fled with care.

The seagulls squawked, they had their say,
As I tripped over and lost my way.
With each sunset, my laughter grew,
While sipping visions of coconut brew.

In twilight hues, memories swell,
All inside my coconut shell.

Footprints in the Sand

I wrote my name with toes so bold,
Then chased a wave, oh how it rolled!
The tide came in with silly glee,
And washed my name as quick as three.

My buddy's footprints, big as boats,
Tried to keep up but lost his hopes.
He stepped on jelly, what a sight,
We screamed and giggled in delight.

The sand buries secrets, it is said,
Like hidden treasures or our bread.
We laughed and followed silly tracks,
While the sun slipped down like playful backs.

Our footprints fade with the setting glow,
But the joy will linger, just like the show.

Conch Shell Serenade

Picked a conch, it looked so grand,
I held it close, heard ocean's band.
Tried to sing but sounded odd,
Like a goat who'd lost the nod.

Friends laughed as I tooted loud,
A goofy tune drew quite a crowd.
We danced around, shells in hands,
Our conch shell concert stole the sands.

The shells chimed in, a crunchy beat,
With every note, we moved our feet.
A crab joined in, he did a jig,
While I laughed so hard, I felt so big.

Under the stars, we serenaded the night,
With conch shell sounds, oh what a fright!

Ghosts of the Beach

At midnight, we heard the waves' sweet call,
Thought we saw ghosts having a ball.
They danced with shadows, such a sight,
We laughed and said, 'Don't give us a fright!'

Sandcastles creaked, they seemed alive,
As we joined in, trying to survive.
The phantom builders with morose laughs,
Played tricks on us, took our photographs.

Flip-flops flung, a wild spree,
Tossed by winds, they tried to flee.
The ghosts just giggled, they had their fun,
'We came to party, let's all run!'

As dawn approached, the fun would cease,
But we swore those ghosts brought us peace.

Moments Captured in Coral

A crab in a hat, what a sight,
Dancing with fish, oh what delight.
Jellyfish glow like disco balls,
They bounce and bounce, and never fall.

Sandy toes and silly grins,
Chasing shells our game begins.
Seagulls squawking, stealing fries,
We laugh until the sun will rise.

Kites in the sky, a colorful spree,
Caught in the wind, like wild and free.
Beach balls bouncing with glee, oh dear,
They land on the head of the lifeguard, I fear!

So here we sit, with laughter bright,
Making memories in the warm sunlight.
Each splash and giggle, captured clear,
A life of fun, we hold so dear.

A Sunset's Farewell

The sun dips low, a giant ball,
Waving bye like it's at a ball.
The ocean winks, with a cheeky splash,
As seagulls dive down in a flashy dash.

Sipping lemonade, don't spill a drop,
Our beachside dance, we just can't stop.
Flip-flops flying, oh what a mess,
Trip on my toes, I must confess!

A sunset smile, painted gold and red,
Fished for memories, don't need a bed.
And just like that, the stars appear,
We laugh at our mishaps, full of cheer.

As the day ends, we wrap it tight,
With giggles and snacks, we say goodnight.
Each flicker of light, a tale to tell,
In this funny world, we know it well.

Crashing Waves and Memories

Waves that crash, like an awkward dance,
Saltwater kisses, and a funny chance.
A seagull swoops, grabs my sandwich tight,
I yell, 'Hey, feathered thief! That's not polite!'

Sandcastles crumble with giggles and care,
A king with a bucket, dripping everywhere.
The tide rolls in to say, 'What's this mess?'
I throw up my hands, 'Just part of the jest!'

Surfboards tumble, folks dive and sway,
Each salty splash brings laughter our way.
A dog in a hat, oh what a sight,
Chasing its tail, in pure delight.

As twilight descends, we gather our dreams,
Beach bonfire flickers, laughter beams.
In every wave, a story unfolds,
Of silly moments and treasures untold.

The Spirit of Tidal Pools

Tidal pools glimmer, creatures so sly,
Starfish grinning, waving goodbye.
A crab wearing glasses, what's that about?
With one silly stare, he's filled with doubt.

Tiny fish dart, playing hide and seek,
While we giggle at their little sneak.
A sea cucumber slips, what a scene,
'They should be careful, they're just too green!'

Giant seaweed, a dance with the breeze,
Tangled up legs, we fall with ease.
Crabs throwing shade like they own the place,
We laugh as we trip on a slippery base.

At the end of the day, we gather our finds,
With shells in our pockets and sandy behinds.
In these natural wonders, laughter runs free,
Life's salty humor is quite the decree!

Tides of Time

Waves are tickling my toes,
Old crabs dance under the sun.
Seagulls squawk with their beaks,
Stealing my fries, oh what fun!

Sandcastles rise, then fall down,
My masterpiece? Just a pile.
Laughter echoes all around,
As we pose for a silly style.

Surfers crash in a grand show,
Trying to ride a rogue wave.
They tumble and twist, oh no!
Land in a splash, so brave.

Time slips by like soggy sand,
Yet our hearts, they remain bright.
With every laugh, a tight hand,
These days, we cherish at night.

Reflections of a Sun-Kissed Heart

Burnt cheeks and salty hair,
Beach ball battles in the air.
Caught a wave, then ate the dirt,
Life's a dance in tan and shirt.

Sandy snacks and fruity drinks,
Laughter shared before it stinks.
Caught a glimpse of my pale feet,
Yikes! A ghost, a feat so sweet!

Flip-flops lost in ocean's churn,
Seashells waiting for my turn.
Tanned and laughing, oh, what glee,
Reflecting who I want to be.

Every sunset brings a cheer,
As we toast with cans of beer.
Those memories so bright, we shout,
For in this life, there's never doubt.

Buried Secrets of the Sand

Digging deep for silver loot,
How I wish for chocolate too!
Instead I find a sock so blue,
Where it's been, I have no clue.

Looking for some buried dough,
But seagulls steal my treasure show.
Peanut butter left behind,
Sticky mess, what will I find?

Old flip-flops, crabs, and shells,
Stories lost that no one tells.
Each grain sings of times gone by,
With every laugh, I wave goodbye.

In the sand, whispers reside,
Wishing I could take a ride.
To dream once more, oh what fun,
From buried secrets, I can run!

Returning to Open Waters

Rowing out with friends in tow,
Splashing water, watch it flow.
Oars in sync, we're quite a show,
Oh look! A dolphin puts on a glow.

Weathered maps and silly tales,
Charting courses, seas and gales.
Who knew we'd drift this far?
Till we hit the nearest bar!

Caught a fish? And made a hat,
It flopped and fell, imagine that!
We laughed so hard, the waves joined in,
As seagulls swooped, ready to win.

Returning back to shore so bold,
With salty hair and stories told.
We'll sail again, Oh what a spree,
With every wave, we'll always be free.

Reflections in the Quiet Lagoon

I saw a fish wearing a hat,
It swam like it owned the flat.
A turtle winked with style so rare,
I laughed so hard, I lost my hair.

The crabs all danced in formal shoes,
While seagulls sang their favorite blues.
A dolphin leaped with quite a flair,
Landing right in my picnic chair.

Norm the pelican stole my fries,
And left me just a sad surprise.
A flamingo tried to raise a toast,
But spilled the drink—oh, what a ghost!

In this lagoon where laughter stays,
Fish wear hats and turtles play.
I'll remember this funny spree,
Where joy and wiggles set us free.

Secrets Cradled in the Waves

The waves told tales of silly things,
Like the time a clam wore fancy rings.
A seaweed dance-off took the place,
Of any fancy ballroom grace.

A whale recited jokes so bad,
His audience was mostly clad.
With flatulent splashes, he did cheer,
While starfish rolled, unable to steer.

A crab in sunglasses strolled right by,
And winked at me with a sly eye.
The ocean's secrets, full of cheer,
Are best shared with a cold cold beer.

With laughter echoing near the shore,
The waves hold secrets and so much more.
Each splash reveals a grin, a sigh,
In this watery world, you must come try!

Recollections of the Distant Surf

I once saw a surfer chase a kite,
That tangled up in his hair, what a sight!
The shrimp in shorts gave him a cheer,
As he face-planted—oh dear, oh dear!

Sandcastles fought a valiant fight,
Against the waves that crashed that night.
A crab with a shovel felt so grand,
But lost his grip and lost the sand.

A pelican tried to steal my drink,
His beak was quick, faster than you think.
With laughter ringing in the salty air,
We all forgot our woes and care.

Recollections made with every splash,
Of goofy scenes that felt like a bash.
In the surf, our joy was true,
Where laughter sparkles, bright and new.

Portrait of a Tranquil Cove

In the cove, I met a gnome,
Who said, 'I'd rather chill than roam.'
He painted seashells, thought it neat,
While crabs danced wildly on their feet.

A fish asked if I'd join his band,
With seaweed guitars, oh so grand.
We played tunes that made the stars twirl,
While dolphins swam and gave a whirl.

A lazy seal took my beach towel,
And snoozed, oh man, what a growl!
As laughter filled the quiet space,
The cove turned into a fun-filled place.

With every wave, a chuckle, a grin,
In that tranquil spot where laughter wins.
The portrait drawn with joy so bright,
Reminds me always to dance with delight.

The Gentle Caress of Ocean Air.

The breeze put my hat on a seagull's head,
As I chased my lunch that swiftly fled.
Sand in my sandwich, a grainy surprise,
I laughed as the gull soared up to the skies.

Flip-flops are flapping, my dance feels quite right,
Until one gets stuck, oh what a delight!
I hop on one foot, the folks start to clap,
As the tide rolls in, I'm caught in the snap.

Surfboards are flailing, it's a comic parade,
One dude takes a tumble, his ego betrayed.
"Catch me some waves!" he calls with a grin,
But ends up swamped by a roll of the din!

So here's to the antics, the laughter so free,
With ocean air carrying fun's jubilee.
As I sip my juice with a big splash of cheer,
I'll treasure these moments, year after year.

Shores of Reflection

Where sunburns and laughter mix with the sand,
My flip-flops have footprints both crooked and grand.
A sandcastle built with a bucket and glee,
Looks more like a monster, oh woe unto me!

Seagulls are stealing my bag of warm fries,
Like thieves in the sunset, they cunningly rise.
I wave my arms wildly, they cackle and flee,
With a chip in their beak, they've outsmarted me!

Swimsuits in stripes and polka dots clash,
In this seaside party, we all make a splash.
A kid with a squirt gun, oh what a delight,
Turns my sunhat to drench-land, a soupy fight!

So here on the shore, where fun knows no bound,
I chuckle at chaos, where joy can be found.
With salty hair flying and hearts full of cheer,
These shores of reflection will pull us near.

Whispering Tides

The waves whisper secrets, they tickle my toes,
While jellyfish wobble in flamboyant clothes.
I dive for a seashell, but find a lost shoe,
The ocean's a joker, it always rings true.

A crabs' conga line marches across the sand,
In their tiny tuxedos, oh isn't it grand?
With a flip and a wiggle, they groove side to side,
I can't help but laugh at their crustacean pride!

Beach balls in action, they fly through the air,
While the old folks just cheer from their portable chairs.
I trip over coolers, my drink takes a dive,
But I'll take this slip as a fun way to thrive!

So here with the tides and their mischievous tease,
Laughter cascades like a refreshing breeze.
Each splash is a giggle, each wave tells a tale,
In this swirl of delight, we'll always prevail.

Echoes of Sunlit Shores

As surfboards topple, the laughter erupts,
Fueled by the folly, our enthusiasm cups.
A beach ball adventures, it floats on the breeze,
Until it nearly knocks over Auntie Louise!

Tanned tourists wobble, attempting to stand,
With flip-flops on feet and drinks in hand.
Their sunburnt expressions, a sight to behold,
As sunglasses slip and their stories unfold!

I spy a good crab with a pinch and a wave,
Looking like he's plotting a scuttle to save.
My snacks on the blanket, he's eyeing them keen,
But then makes a getaway, all swift and unseen!

So here on these shores where the echoes resound,
With friends all around, and laughter profound.
We'll dance with the sand and play silly games,
In the echoes of sunlit shores, joy reigns.

The Coral Heartbeat

In sunlit days, we danced with glee,
Where fish wore shades, wild and free.
A crab in shades stole my flip-flop,
With a wink, then scuttled, never to stop.

We swam with dolphins, quite a sight,
Till one gave chase, I took flight!
But laughter echoed in salty air,
As I floundered, splashed without a care.

A parrot squawked, my drink he stole,
As we lounged on the warm, sandy shoal.
He toasted with juice, a cheeky toast,
"Cheers to the sand and moonlight boast!"

With coral tunes and sunlit fun,
We'll treasure these days when day is done.

Lost Horizons

We set sail past waves of foam,
On a boat that was never our home.
With the map upside down, oh what a fuss,
We ended up lost; blame the bus?

The seagulls laughed, they knew the trick,
As we bobbed and weaved and danced the stick.
A treasure chest? Just some old cans,
But we still felt like wealthy fans.

With instant noodles, we feasted bright,
Reigning champs of the 'dinner' fight.
A coconut fell, right on my head,
"Now this is a 'nutty' way to be fed!"

At dusk we laughed, let care drift away,
Lost but happy, under stars' ballet.

Found Dreams

On a beach where sandcastles grow,
We found a flip-flop, a prize for show.
It had a story, as all things do,
Of a beach bum wearing just one shoe.

We tossed a frisbee, missed a catch,
It flew off like a runaway batch.
Landed in a crab's evening feast,
He waved at us, "Not for the least!"

With ice cream dripping, we painted skies,
Each scoop a color of our alibis.
A seagull swooped, snatched my cone,
Life's delicious, even when alone.

Together we laughed, on this bright scheme,
Chasing the shadows of silly dreams.

Moonlit Paths on Serene Waters

Under the moon, we rowed the night,
A rubber duck led our silly flight.
It quacked a tune, we sang along,
Our boat might sink, but the fun was strong.

The stars shone bright, like disco balls,
As we splashed loudly, heedless of falls.
With a wink and grin from a fish nearby,
"Join the party, don't be shy!"

A turtle winked, gave us a wave,
"Keep it down, I'm trying to save."
But we just chuckled, in the moonlit glow,
Laughing in ripples, our joy on show.

So we paddled on, till the dawn did peep,
With dreams of quacks drifting into sleep.

Treasures of the Forgotten Cove

Deep in the cove, where secrets hide,
We found an old shoe, on the tide.
"My treasure," I claimed with a silly grin,
For what's more fun than a worn-out win?

We dug in the sand for pearls of delight,
Found a bottle! It wasn't polite.
A message inside? Just a shopping list,
"Milk, eggs, and fun" — how could I resist?

A surfboard wedged in the rocks just right,
"We'll ride this wave, come day or night!"
But when I tried, I fell with a splat,
Even the seagulls laughed at that!

Yet here we would stay, treasure seekers bold,
With laughter and stories worth more than gold.

Shells of Time

In pockets, sand grains cling tight,
A hermit crab steals my flip-flop flight.
Seagulls squawk, my sandwich they claim,
Laughter erupts, oh what a shame!

Footprints lead, then vanish fast,
Where did they go? Such a blast!
Barefoot dancing, I slip and slide,
The tide chuckles, I sit in pride.

Shells tell stories of sun and fun,
Tales of sunburns, oh what a run!
Snorkels forgotten, underwater dreams,
Surfboards flipping—quite ridiculous schemes!

As the sun dips low, we make a toast,
Here's to the laughter we love the most.
With each wave crashing, joy won't cease,
In this sandy paradise, our spirits increase.

An Ode to Coral Gardens

Beneath the waves, fish dance and spin,
Bright corals giggle, where do I begin?
Clumsy divers with gear all askew,
Splashing in rhythms both silly and true.

Sea turtles glide, kings of the deep,
While I unintentionally take a leap.
Bubbles escape with every chortle,
Do they laugh too? Under the coral.

A jellyfish wobbles, we swim right past,
Its graceful jig is a sight so vast.
Octopus thinking, "Who wears this look?"
Even his ink becomes a hook!

When the sun sets low, the water glows bright,
We chase the fish under stars of night.
With each splash we echo, joy we expand,
Together we laugh in this sea-covered land.

The Memory of Saltwater Tears

A wave crashes down, what a surprise!
With salty spray, it blinds my eyes.
I stumble back, laughter erupts,
It's just the ocean and its silly hiccups.

Seashells collected, but where's my hat?
A gust of wind—oh, this is quite the spat!
I chase after it, stumbling so wild,
Like a toddler in tan, so uncouth and riled.

Saltwater pools, they gather around,
Like memories shared with friends who abound.
In this chaos, joy finds a way,
Each drop that falls brings wild play.

As the tide ebbs, we wipe the tears,
The laughter we share wipes away the fears.
In silly moments, we find our delight,
Wrapped in the tide, everything feels right.

Beneath the Palms

Beneath the palms, where shadows play,
I swing too hard, then fly away.
Landing in sand, what a funny sight,
Even the crabs give me a fright!

Coconuts drop with an echoing thud,
Sending us running, giggles in the mud.
A game of dodge, as dusk turns to glow,
It's a comedy show, all part of the show.

Sunburnt noses, we paint them bright,
Rainbow hues in the soft fading light.
The breeze whispers secrets of day's delight,
We share hearty laughter beneath the twilight.

As stars twinkle down, the night does reside,
Under the palms, we take it all in stride.
With every giggle, memories rewind,
A tapestry woven of fun, unconfined.

Windswept Tales of Nostalgia

A seagull stole my sandwich, oh what a plight,
I chased him around, in the fading sunlight.
With my hat blown off and my shoes in a mess,
I laughed as I tripped, in my sandy distress.

The tide brought in treasures, a flip-flop or two,
My friend found a jellyfish, which turned out to be glue.
We crafted fine jewelry from seaweed and shells,
Yet wore them with pride, in our laughter it dwells.

The beach ball exploded, with a loud, shocking pop,
We all took a dive, in the nearby soda shop.
Gelato for lunch? What a daring affair,
We giggled and slurped, with ice cream in hair.

As the sun began setting, we danced on the shore,
In flip-flops and goggles, we laughed ever more.
With rays painting skies in a sunset so bright,
Windswept tales linger, a pure heartfelt delight.

Sunswept Days and Starry Nights

Woke up to confusion, where's my other shoe?
Last seen with a crab, or was it my cousin Lou?
The sun beamed down, like a giant golden ball,
We toasted with coconuts, feeling ten feet tall.

The surfboards were wobbly, and so were we,
Tumbling through waves, like fish out of tea.
One fell off his board and yelled with a laugh,
"I'm just practicing how to improve my calve!"

Nights under the stars, we'd roast marshmallows,
While telling tales of ghosts and how they throw pillows.
Each crunch was a giggle, each pop was a cheer,
"Is that a ghost, or just the sound of your beer?"

The moon took our pictures, with beams shinning wide,
We danced like wild mariners, with no sense of pride.
Each moment a treasure, and with laughter so bright,
We basked in our joys, under sunswept nights.

The Color of Oceanic Reverie

Oh, the sea was like a canvas, bright blue and bold,
With crab-shaped paintbrushes, our stories unfold.
We splashed colors and giggles, more fun than a play,
While chasing our toes, as they sank in the bay.

The wind played confetti, in our tangled hair,
While fish jumped in rhythms, with flair beyond compare.

Our laughter echoed louder, like seagulls at play,
We painted the ocean, one splash at a spray!

We built castles of sand, with moats full of dreams,
Each wave brought more laughs, or so it seems.
Then a rogue wave came in, knocked down our great wall,

We just built it back up, oh how we had a ball!

As the sun dipped below, painted skies in a dance,
We shared stories of pirates and took off our pants!
In colors of chuckles, our hearts full of cheer,
A gallery of joy, that we hold ever dear.

A Shell's Secret Keep

I found a small shell, and urged it to talk,
It told me of secrets in rocks and on dock.
With whispers of seaweed, it chattered away,
"I've seen seagulls dance, oh, what a wild display!"

My friend claimed a conch, held to her ear tight,
All she heard was her giggles, what a silly sight!
"Tell me a secret!" she begged of the shell,
"It only says 'Keep laughing', and that's just swell!"

We gathered them all, this peculiar crew,
Each shell held a story, of dreams old and new.
"Let's start a museum!" I boldly declared,
"A wacky collection of laughter we shared!"

As the sun kissed the horizon, we stacked our great finds,
In a pile of pure joy, with mischief aligned.
We promised to cherish, these treasures we'd seek,
For the laughter we shared, was our shell's secret keep.

Forgotten Footprints on the Beach

Footprints in the sand so wide,
Left by folks who laughed and cried.
One slip, two trips, a splash like a fish,
We chased the waves, oh, what a wish!

Seagulls cackled, they had a blast,
As we stumbled forward, running fast.
But who knew sand could be so sly?
A flip, a flop, then a sudden cry!

Our snacks were buried, a great escapade,
While crabs scuttled off with the lemonade.
Tanned and toasted, we wore our glee,
With shells for trophies, just wait and see!

Laughing loudly, our voices soared,
With silly stories, we never bored.
So cheers to footprints, silly and sweet,
In the sun's warm hug, we danced on our feet!

A Breeze of Remembered Laughter

A breeze tickled noses, what fun it did bring,
As we chased after kites made of string.
We spun in circles, arms wide like birds,
And slipped on the grass with our silly words.

The sun gave a wink in the sky so blue,
As we tossed water balloons—we knew what to do!
Direct hits and giggles filled the bright air,
We squelched through puddles without a care.

With beach hats askew and snacks piled high,
We swatted away those pesky flies.
We leaned back and laughed at the world,
Swirling in memories as laughter unfurled.

Then came an ice cream truck with a jingle so sweet,
We raced like the wind, oh, what a treat!
With sticky fingers and faces aglow,
In the breeze of our laughter, we let our hearts flow!

Beneath the Palms of Yesterday

Beneath old palms, our secrets lay,
Where dreams were formed in the light of day.
We'd play our games with sticks and stones,
And laughed at the crabs with their little tones.

A coconut fell—what a hilarious sight!
It dropped with a thud; we took to flight!
We built tiny castles, they crumbled in glee,
As tides laughed at us, so wild and free.

We'd spin tales of pirates and treasure chests,
With giggles erupting, we were truly blessed.
From sunup to sundown, the fun never waned,
As we danced in the shade, our spirits unchained.

And when the stars peeked, our laughter would rise,
Swirling in secrets beneath midnight skies.
The palm trees swayed with a knowing grin,
In the heart of our laughter, forever we'd win!

The Chime of Distant Bells

The chime of bells drifted through the breeze,
Reminding us of days with sand on our knees.
Silly hats wobbling, we danced out of tune,
With fishy puns and a laugh like a loon.

In the distance, the waves said hello,
As we raced with the tide for a splashy show.
The beach umbrellas were our jolly stage,
While we performed antics for the gulls to gauge.

Our sunburnt noses were badges of pride,
As we dodged flying frisbees that came from the side.
Oh, the sound of the giggles, a symphony bright,
As we chased down our ice creams, pure delight!

So here's to those chimes, like laughter they ring,
In the heart of our stories, joy's always king.
With salty embraces and friends by our side,
Forever we'll treasure this fun-filled ride!

Beneath the Coconut Trees

Underneath the tall green trees,
I spotted some buzzing bees.
They danced around my coconut drink,
I swatted them fast, but they wouldn't blink.

A parrot perched with sass so bright,
Challenged me to a dance, what a sight!
I twirled and tripped on my flip-flop shoe,
The bird just laughed, and I laughed too.

With a splash and a giggle, I fell in the sand,
The sun was hot, and my sunscreen was bland.
I roasted like chicken, my laughter was loud,
While crabs scuttled by, looking quite proud.

The drinks were cold; I gave a toast,
To hungry fish, we bloated like ghosts.
But who could complain when the breeze was right?
We danced with the palms till the fall of night.

Lost in the Azure

In a sea of blue where I lost my hat,
It floated away like a rebellious cat.
I yelled, 'Come back!' but it swam out of sight,
The seagulls around me began their flight.

A fish popped up with a cheeky grin,
Teasing my hat like, 'What a fun spin!'
I splashed in the waves, but oh what a blunder,
Caught in a wave, I fell like thunder.

A dolphin winked and gave me a show,
While I made friends with a crab down below.
He pinched my toe, saying, 'Hey, that's not cool!'
Webbed with laughter, we splashed in the pool.

Finally emerged with my squishy crown,
Wrung out my clothes, felt like a clown.
But with sun on my face and salt in my hair,
I chuckled, 'Next time, I'll just wear a spare!'

Sand Between My Toes

Woke up to find a sandcastle high,
Built by my friends who were quite spry.
With moats and towers, it looked like a dream,
But I tripped on a shell, and oh! What a scream!

Seagulls took turns stealing our snacks,
We threw breadcrumbs to defend our packs.
Amidst the chaos of feathery threats,
We planned our revenge with tinfoil nets.

Footprints behind me were a tale of dread,
As I waddled along, my flip-flops led.
The sand was warm; it stuck to my feet,
Every step forward brought laughter and heat.

With a volley of laughter, we ran for the sea,
Splashing and tumbling, feeling so free.
Through the giggles and splashes, we held on tight,
Counting our treasures, what a wild sight!

The Laughter of Waves

The waves crashed and roared with a chuckle,
They pulled at my toes like a playful struggle.
I yelled, 'Not today!' but they just laughed back,
I stumbled and fell, in a watery snack.

Caught in a swirl, I surfed on my belly,
Like a walrus in training, oh so silly!
Friends on the beach just couldn't stop howling,
As I rode in circles and kept doing my bowing.

A sand crab joined in on my dance,
Clapping his claws, giving it a chance.
We spun like wild with no care in our hearts,
Drawing onlookers—now that was the art!

As the sun slipped low, painting skies so bright,
I waved goodbye to the waves, what a sight!
With giggles echoing under the wide sky,
The ocean whispered, 'We'll meet again, bye!'

Drifted Hearts by the Sea

We danced with crabs on the wet sand,
Sipping coconut juice, feeling quite grand.
A seagull stole our fries with a screech,
Chasing it down like we were on the beach.

The tide came in, our shoes went out,
Chasing after fish, we jumped about.
Our laughter echoed over the waves,
While a jellyfish wobbled, oh how it misbehaves!

We built a castle with moats and dreams,
Until the tide laughed and burst our seams.
With sand in our hair, and salt on our feet,
We'd play all day, till the sunset's sweet.

Now those moments, like tides, ebb and flow,
In the corner of my heart, they glow.
With every wave that rolls ashore,
I chuckle at the antics we adore.

Reminiscing in the Sea Breeze

The wind playfully tousled our hair,
As we raced each other without a care.
With boogie boards bobbing, we fell with a splash,
Oh, those ocean battles—what a funny clash!

Finding seashells, we thought we were rich,
But half were just rocks, oh what a hitch!
We named each one as a treasure so grand,
While seagulls conspired, plotting their stand.

Every crab we met, a little wise guy,
Scuttling away as we'd start to pry.
Chasing them down, we'd end on the ground,
With giggles and bruises, laughter abound.

Now I reminisce with a chuckle and sigh,
As the sea breeze whispers, a soft lullaby.
In the mist of those days, we danced so free,
In that world of laughter beneath the sea.

Sunkissed Horizons

On the shores where the sun kissed our toes,
We built our dreams in the sand where it flows.
Each grain of time held a giggle or two,
As we splashed through puddles of salty hue.

The sunburned art on our backs, such a sight,
Like badly painted canvases, oh what a fright!
With ice cream melting faster than we could bite,
Our sticky fingers led to a comedic plight.

On this stage of goofiness, we played our part,
With flip-flops flying, we'd break our own heart.
Every wave crashing felt like a cheer,
For our silly adventures as summer drew near.

Now the horizon whispers sweet tales of glee,
Of laughter and friendship by the bright sea.
With every sunset, those memories don't cease,
In our hearts, they'll dance—what a time, oh what peace!

Waves of the Past

In the surf where we splashed like rambunctious kids,
We dared each other, "C'mon, let's flip off the skids!"
With each tumble in waves, we laughed till we cried,
As the ocean cheered on, swaying side to side.

Collecting sea glass, thinking we'd score,
Trading our finds, like pirate folklore.
But the only treasure was the way that we'd share,
Those moments of joy, caught up in the air.

We adorned ourselves with seaweed for style,
Strutting like models, but more like a mile.
With crabs as our audience, we were the toast,
Of every sandbar, raising laughter's proud boast.

Now waves whisper secrets of fun in the night,
Reminding us gently of those moments so bright.
With every splash of the tide's lively dance,
We see through the years, lost in our prance.

Hummingbird Whispers

A tiny bird flits by with a grin,
Whispering secrets of where it has been.
It sips from the flowers, a dazzling sight,
Chasing its shadow in the warm morning light.

The breeze lifts my hat, takes it for a spin,
While I trip on my flip-flops, oh where to begin?
Laughing at seagulls, so snappy and bold,
Trading their fish for some silver and gold.

A splash from a wave gives me quite the fright,
Dancing seafoam makes the whole scene so bright.
The beach ball's escaped, it's soaring away,
While I'm pondering lunch and what I might pay.

With seashells for pockets, I stroll by the shore,
Collecting my treasures, always wanting more.
The sun dips low, shadows start to tease,
A day like this, surely, will never cease.

Twilight Reflections on Water

The sky wears colors not meant for a hat,
While frogs serenade in a chorus of chat.
I sit on a log, the water's buttery sheen,
Known only to ducks who float like a dream.

I throw in my worries, they sink without trace,
While fish laugh and swim in a bewitching race.
The fireflies blink like they're trying to text,
I swear this evening is totally perplexed.

Grandma's old stories hover in the trees,
About a brave pirate who danced with the bees.
His treasure was laughter, the booty was joy,
Though he lost all his gold playing cards with a boy.

As twilight sneaks in, I chuckle and sigh,
Even the stars seem to wink at the sky.
With memories painted in each crafty light,
I nestle my heart, all snug for the night.

Sailing into Yesterday

A boat made of dreams and a pinch of delight,
Set sail on the waves, what a whimsical flight!
My compass is broken, it points to the sun,
While I navigate laughter and tales of pure fun.

With seagulls as crew, they squawk out a tune,
Charting our course by the light of the moon.
Each wave a reminder, each splash a new cheer,
Like a silly old movie, we smile ear to ear.

Oh look, there's a fish presenting its dance,
While I giggle so hard that I nearly lose my pants!
The gulls are auditioning, they take to the stage,
As I clap and I cheer from the bow of my page.

We sail into yesterday, not lost but alive,
With treasures of laughter that help us survive.
The wind whispers secrets, the sea roars with glee,
As I wave at the sun, my heart feels so free.

The Heartbeat of the Ocean

The ocean beats softly, like a drum made of foam,
With each gentle wave, I feel right at home.
Crabs waddle by wearing their best,
Dressed up for a party, they rarely get stressed.

The shells gossip secrets, so grand and so bold,
Of past underwater treasures, lost gems and gold.
I sit by the sands, as the tides play a tune,
While flocks of sea turtles glide past on a swoon.

A jellyfish floats by, glowing bright like a lamp,
Giving me side-eye, oh what a strange champ!
I laugh at their jigs, their wobbly ballet,
Claiming the title of 'Best Dance' today.

As sunset erupts in a grand burst of cheer,
I wish for this laughter to always stay near.
The heartbeat is strong, in this place I adore,
With tides full of giggles, forever and more.

Laughter Amongst the Tides

The crabs dance sideways, quite absurd,
They steal your sandwich without a word.
A seagull squawks, 'You think you're sly!'
While rich ol' fish just swims on by.

Flip-flops fly in the breeze with flair,
As we play tag with the salty air.
A wind gust laughs, 'Catch me if you can!'
But we roll in the sand, every goofy man.

Grandma's sunhat turns into a kite,
Bobbing and weaving, oh what a sight!
We chase it down, our laughter loud,
As it flirts with clouds, so proud, so proud!

At sunset's glow, we tell tales tall,
Of fish that jumped and crabs that crawl.
With giggles and chuckles, the night takes flight,
'Til the stars wink down, it's a funny night!

Sunbeams Through the Mangrove

The trees wear shades, 'cause they're so cool,
Old man Jenkins claims he's "the pool's jewel".
A pelican dives; flops! What a clatter,
We laugh so hard, what's that? Oh, a splatter!

Tiki torches whip up a breeze,
Slipping on conch shells with perfect ease.
A crab gives chase, and what a debate,
Who'll have the last fry? And who's gained weight?

Riding waves on a floaty swan,
The neighbor's cat tries to join the fun.
With all of us giggling, what can we say?
'This cat's got style, in a very strange way!'

Sunbeams flicker, as laughter flows,
Through twisted roots, where the green grass grows.
With cheeky grins and merry shouts,
We'll dance 'til the night, that's what it's about!

Salt and Time: A Journey Back

Gather 'round the beach bonfire's glow,
With stories of pirates, and a lost toe!
The fish that got away, oh what a tale,
With twists and turns, like a clumsy whale.

A time capsule buried in the sand,
Contains a flip-flop and a crusty hand.
We giggle and snicker, as secrets unfold,
While another bad joke, we lovingly told.

Tales of the seagulls and their bold theft,
That poor sandwich, we'll never forget.
With salt in the air and crumbs on our face,
We toast to laughter, all over the place!

As waves lap gently, like a calming balm,
We reminisce the days, all in high charm.
With wishes whispered to the rising tide,
We laugh at the past, with joy by our side!

Tales from the Driftwood Promenade

Wandering down where the driftwood lies,
We stumbled upon some flotsam surprise.
A parrot squawks, 'You're late for a show!'
While we gather shells, with sand in tow.

Old beach chairs turned into artful thrones,
Claiming kingship over seaweed and stones.
A child's laugh echoes, so pure, and free,
Chasing waves like a wild jubilee.

At sunset's edge, shells tell stories grand,
Of starfish ballads and life's quirky band.
We hold hands tightly, then twist into a run,
As gulls squabble overhead, oh what fun!

So here we stand, on this sun-kissed land,
With driftwood tales and a heart always fanned.
Our laughter a melody, the sea our friend,
In this fine adventure, there's no end!

Hazy Days of Golden Light

On sandy shores where crabs parade,
I lost my flip-flop in the shade.
The seagulls laughed, they took a dive,
While I danced on, trying to jive.

With sunburned noses, we made a pact,
To catch some waves, but we lost the act.
A kite took flight, our lunch on tow,
Now fish are feasting, what a show!

A sunscreen battle, we smeared and laughed,
My friend claims he's stuck, what a craft!
We played all day, 'til light turned gray,
Chasing shadows, with jokes on replay.

As the final sunset winked goodbye,
We flipped a coin, it flew too high.
Caught in bushes, with giggling glee,
Those hazy days were wild and free!

The Dance of Morning Dew

Morning brought a shiny prize,
Grass so wet, it looked like pies.
We slipped and slid, like clumsy fools,
Our laughter echoed, breaking rules.

Glimmers sparkled on our toes,
"Hey, look! A snail!" my brother goes.
It zoomed away with quite a flair,
Chasing it led us everywhere!

We twirled like leaves in bright sunlight,
Splashing puddles, joyous delight.
But then I tripped—oh what a sight!
A dance of dew turned into fright!

As shadows lengthened, giggles waned,
A treasure hunt for shoes, we gained.
With morning's tale tucked neat and few,
We'll always cherish the dance of dew.

Bottled Memories of The Depths

We ventured forth to find lost things,
In crystal waves where laughter rings.
A bottle gleamed, we pulled it near,
Expecting treasures, Oh, my dear!

Inside the glass, a note unspooled,
"Help! I'm stuck—please send a pool!"
We cackled hard, as waves did swell,
The ocean's pranks, they knew it well.

Old flip-flops danced through coral beds,
Jellyfish bounced off kids' hot heads.
Each splash a cheer, concert in foam,
Who knew the sea could feel like home?

With tales tucked tight in salty hair,
We returned with sand to spare.
In memories sealed, our hearts all crept,
Beneath the sun, where laughter leapt.

The Colors of Dusk

As day bid farewell with a cheeky grin,
We painted skies with orange and kin.
A cupcake bird fluffed its bright plume,
Cheering as shadows began to loom.

We chased the sun, ran like the wind,
Looking for treasure, a game to begin.
With each sunset, wild stories spun,
Of pirates lost, and treasures won.

Napping crabs tucked in for the night,
While we built castles, quite a sight!
But waves snickered, washed them away,
"Next time," we said, "we'll plan a stay!"

The colors of dusk, they whispered low,
Tales of mischief in this glow.
As stars peeped out, one by one,
We vowed to return, when day was done!

Lighthouses and Legends

There once was a tower, so tall and bright,
Its light played hide and seek every night.
The seagulls complained, they thought it was rude,
To shine on their fish, it messed with their food.

A captain once swore he spotted a ghost,
Dancing by the beam, he ran, yelling 'Host!'
But all it turned out was a mop and a broom,
Their nightly cleaning crew, clearing the gloom.

With every tall tale, we'd laugh till we cried,
Of a crab that wore glasses and a fish that had lied.
For every old legend born of the sea,
Was just another joke shared by you and me.

So let the waves chuckle and the wind do its jest,
In tales of the lighthouse, we found our best quest.
With humor so bright, like the sun on a sail,
We'll keep telling stories, we're destined to fail!

Whispered Secrets of the Coast

The whispers of shells hold secrets untold,
Of crabs that tell stories, both silly and bold.
They giggle at tides that come and retreat,
And argue about who makes the best treat.

One starfish claimed it could dance like a pro,
While a clam just sat grumpy, said 'No, no, no!'
They painted the sand with tales made of glee,
Of fish who wore hats, and swam up a tree.

Seagulls would swoop in, piping their two cents,
While we all just laughed at the nonsense events.
With each wave that rolled in, new jokes would arise,
In the theater of coastlines, we wore our disguise.

So here's to the secrets that make us all grin,
The coast has its charm, let the laughter begin.
In this salty surrounds, where funny tales boast,
We cherish those moments, dear friends, toast a toast!

Misty Mornings and Sweet Goodbyes

In the morning mist, as the sun sits in doubt,
We'd trip over driftwood, and laugh as we shout.
A crab on the shore waved a funny ol' claw,
While we cringed at that sight, then cheered with a paw.

Our boats were either floating or stuck in the sand,
With oars made of rubber, it was never quite planned.
The tide crept on in, bringing laughter anew,
As we shouted our goodbyes to the picnic and brew.

With seabreeze so fickle, it tossed us about,
Somehow we lost all the snacks, made us pout.
Yet we found our delight in the birds' merry strut,
Though we missed our sandwiches, ah, luck, what a rut!

So we'll hold onto moments beneath skies so wide,
With each wet smirk and laugh, we let joy be our guide.
Through foggy escapades and soft tides that sigh,
We'll treasure these mornings and sweet, sweet goodbye!

The Lure of Untouched Shores

There's magic in sand, said the flip-flop and sock,
Who argued and grumbled, 'Don't you dare block!'
With a wink and a nudge, they formed a parade,
And led us to shores where the fun never strayed.

The sea churned and bubbled with giggles and glee,
As clams threw a party, inviting the bee.
With seaweed confetti, they danced on the tide,
While we tried catching laughter that looped far and wide.

And yet as we splashed through the waters so warm,
A crab in a tux said, 'Was this the norm?'
We laughed at the question, and cheered with delight,
It's simply a day that feels perfectly right!

So here's to the shores that call us to play,
With friends made of sand and some seaweed bouquet.
The lure is so strong, as each wave rolls ashore,
We'll chase after laughter, forever wanting more!

www.ingramcontent.com/pod-product-compliance
Lightning Source LLC
Chambersburg PA
CBHW072217070526
44585CB00015B/1374